Graphic Scenes

Also by Randy Blasing

Randy Blasing

GRAPHIC SCENES

Persea Books / New York

Grateful acknowledgment is made to the editors of the magazines that first published certain of these poems: *The Literary Review* ("Second Language"), *Michigan Quarterly Review* ("The Sky as the Limit"), *The Nation* ("Faded Kodachrome"), *The New Criterion* ("Hardball"), *The Paris Review* ("Hymn to the Sun"), *Poet & Critic* ("Color Values," "Setting Out"), *Poetry* ("Burial Grounds," "Lifelines," "Permanent Ink," "Mother Tongue," "Chambers of the Heart," "Man of Letters," "Cardiogram," "At Length"), *The Sewanee Review* ("Country Song," "Visionary Company"), *The South Florida Poetry Review* ("Dark Matter"), and *The Southern Review* ("Star Island," "Personal History").

I wish to thank the Ingram Merrill Foundation for their generous support, which helped me greatly to complete this book.—R.B.

Library of Congress Cataloging-in-Publication Data
Blasing, Randy.
    Graphic scenes : poems / Randy Blasing.
        p. cm.
    ISBN 0-89255-202-6 : $10.00
    I. Title.
    PS3552.L38G73   1994
    811'.54—dc20

                                          94-8736
                                            CIP

Set in Galliard by Louis Giardini
Manufactured in the United States of America
First Edition

for Mutlu

These things at least comprise
An occupation, an exercise, a work . . .

Wallace Stevens

CONTENTS

I

SOURCES

For a long time I had no memory,
no feeling for the Mother of the Muses,
but first geography (retracing journeys
I made under my parents' tutelage
to Upper Michigan & Rapid City)
& then history (growing up every inch
of the way under a dark cloud that mushroomed
in dreams) slowly awakened me to looking
over my shoulder & imagining
the days that brought me here, like stepping stones
I found at Lake Itasca as an up-
a-creek Tenderfoot getting my feet wet
breaking my own path back toward the source
—all the signs read—of the Father of Waters.

COLOR VALUES

The trees go to blazes—cranberry swamp
maples, pumpkin birches, honey
sycamores. Once the sun
peaked in June, it was all downhill
into the fire for them, & in the spirit

of fall I burn to see myself at ten
shoulder again my uncle's double-barreled
twelve-gauge my father had me point
at a gilded oak's lowest branch
off the Cass Lake road, my black Labrador

frozen in her tracks & my mother's voice
a whisper coaching me
not to pull but squeeze the trigger: one blast
reduced a family of partridges
to dust. Looking at what I'd done

with buckshot, I had seen enough to last
a lifetime, doomed as I believed I was
when I found their minute pin
feathers delicately tinged
cinnamon, as if someone loved them also.

BALANCE SHEET

1. MATERIAL CULTURE

On a Turkish flat-weave the yellow, red,
& orange all the maple trees have changed,
I run across a working spinning wheel
for sale under a First Baptist steeple

needling the blue. Suddenly I can hear
my father calling me a wool-gatherer
again, afraid I'll take to spinning yarns
& undo him by not bringing home bacon

as a man. Every English teacher swears
I lack imagination, but I've learned
heaven is here & now if I'm a maker.

I tap my foot as if against the cold
& go in circles that come out straight lines,
threading my way back to my father's house.

2. FLEA MARKET

To my surprise I find beneath the dust
spools of the Belding Corticelli thread
("Since 1832") my father supplied
notions buyers all across the Upper
Midwest, back when women like my mother
eyed the right shade of his mercerized cotton
to piece their clothes together seamlessly.

I follow this thread into the labyrinth
to where my father stayed up late on Sundays
& filled out reports of his expenses
as if his company could pay the cost
of three-week business trips away from home,
the way settling my account with the past
only amounts to adding up my losses.

STAR ISLAND

At last they've reached the Golden Isles, where no
such thing as weather singles out the days

& nights are just the necessary pauses
between breaths, none of which will necessarily

last forever. In this or that one pacing
the shore where they, the saved & saving, have come

to stay, where a dead stick becomes a quick
chameleon, a lion's-paw a fallen

autumn leaf, or any of the wind-beached
palm fronds a washed-up fish's skeleton,

I see my parents as they might have been:
themselves in bronze, surviving their own lives.

FAMILY PLOT

1. IN THE BLOOD

I come from a family of big hearts:
my father's oversize from lettering
in four sports in high school & college,
my mother's also swollen after winning
not a game but a battle with rheumatic
fever that scarred her for life, & mine one-
fourth again its normal fist-size from marching
out of step, speeded-up as if racing

with time. My mother's last picture finds her
smiling outside her Florida apartment
but shrugging her left shoulder like my father
at the end, as though her own heavy heart's
about to burst. Reading my fate in theirs,
I unburden my full heart as I go.

2. MEMORIAL PROPERTY

Now, in the dark of winter, there's a letter
from Highland Gardens down in Winter Park,
Florida lowlands where a slab flush
with the earth stands for my mother, who survives

on paper in my heart. Thirty years back,
she wore red to my father's funeral
on Valentine's, their anniversary.

February leads the months in losses
per diem, I am fatefully informed,
& heaven knows I should nail down a space

for myself soon. The heart does all the thinking,
those masters of death the ancient Egyptians
believed, & I will put my name instead
on this snowbound plot, buried with my dead.

PERSONAL HISTORY

A four-letter pre-med grad the Crash plunged
into selling Louisiana Northrup
King seed & Iowa J&J's
wonder drugs before he earned his commission

& shipped out for the war, my father wound
up a "rag" man—his grandfather had been
a tailor until, setting sail from Hamburg
for Minnesota land, he joined the Union

Army—& thus steered me toward German
classes for their value to the doctor
I, at least, would be, but when blue-eyed Miss
Snabbi (her given name, Grace, off-limits)

read us eternal sophomores Wolfgang Borchert
& Gottfried Benn, who in their words
sifted through the ashes
of a future gone up in smoke,

the spirit of the letters she translated
dovetailed with my sense I would burn
tomorrow, my name written down
with the black mark of having life too good

against it in the Book, & I began
to dream not of escaping fate
but of rewriting it to make it mine:
just as my German family name sounded

English to me—I can still hear my father
telling somebody on the phone, "It's *Blazing*
but with an *s*"—I would find my own way
into the flames.

DARK MATTER

Once more in my experience, jonquils
risen from leaden ground trumpet the gold
of everlasting life, while higher up
a bee fat as my thumb but black & yellow
like the throats of light-eating tulips scarlet
as Japan's rising sun
feels the pull of each five-pointed white giant
exploding into view on my celestial

pair of apple trees. In their shadow the scent
of lilies of the valley rings a bell
with me & calls me back
to the dark bed outside my mother's house,
where I lived until I was a good two
& my kamikaze'd father got shipped
home in the light of all those suns dawning
on Nagasaki & Hiroshima.

SUNDAY SCHOOL

We'd just moved into our first house—a white
"crackerbox," my mother would have christened it
if it weren't ours, with trim as deep a blue
as my dad's '46 Olds with the latest,
the earliest automatic transmission
I saw from the plush back seat flabbergast
my grandfather on a road of sun-silvered
poplars at three—when my parents dropped me

at Sunday school. I still picture them lounging
around at home without me, the *Star* filling
up the room like drifted snow shot with soot
from the coal furnace down where the iceman
left his calling card each time he delivered:
piss in the drain. But soon the minister
drew the line at babysitting me
& told them to join up or keep me home

next Sunday morning. Five years & two
houses later, I entered a church basement
that suffered little children & let grown-
ups ascend to the pine-&-glass chapel
overhead. I listened to my teacher
extoll the shocking, invisible power
of electricity, his specialty,
& we kids passed around artists' impressions

of the Holy Land—donkeys, olive trees,
& coats of many colors—in the room
where women decanted the Welch's grape juice
the elders substituted for the wine
it went against their religion to serve
at Communion, a cube of Wonder Bread
stuck in each throat. Until I graduated
upstairs, I did five years of worshiping

the ground under my feet (brown squares flecked white,
like giant-size Hershey bars forgotten
in our gas-cooled Hotpoint). Once a Life Scout,
I raised countless First- & Second-Class drowning

victims up from the dead by kneeling down
on that cold shore & chanting under my breath
Out goes the bad air, in comes the good air
like a spell. Staring down the congregation

at thirteen, before the sunrise service
ended with the customary prayer
for the health of President Eisenhower,
I read verses from St. Paul's Ephesus
chapter, suddenly in love with the letters
I found clustered on bread-white Bible leaves
like black Concord grapes, & I rolled them around
on my tongue without thinking what they meant

beyond their shape & sound. It was the body
of words that I desired, & I partook
of them as if they were the flesh & blood
of the spirit that gave me life, because
they translated—when, in due time, they came
from me—the world into my terms & made
a place in it for me at last, a likely
story I imagined for myself.

CHAMBERS OF THE HEART

Since I know by heart the floor plan
of every house I grew up in,
I follow in my own footsteps

& enter the living room now of house
number two, where I re-shot with cap guns
our first TV's Saturday-morning version

of Custer's last stand to my satisfaction,
& my father zoomed in on the small screen
to size up big-talking Joe McCarthy.

When, in the dining L, my mother lunched
with girlfriends winter afternoons, I played
alone under the table, in the five

o'clock shadow of all those legs. The hall
between the bedrooms framed my silhouette
snipped out at Dayton's in a flash, eyelashes

intact. Just as I made the rounds of past
houses, memorizing their ins & outs
like someone going blind, I move, as though

by plan, from room to room on this blueprint,
still a black figure on a light background,
& measure off my future home.

CURTAIN

When I last visited my mother's house,
only her scent remained of her, Estee
rising from her bureau drawers & clinging
to what she always called her "outfits" lined
up in her closet like suits on parade.
A torch singer in her youth, she'd performed
all her life, making a spectacle

of every day. Invisible, she hovered
in the air of her one-bedroom, & I slept
on her hard, living-room convertible
instead of stretching out between the sheets
in the icy single where she'd come to grief,
her bedside oxygen holding its breath.
Everywhere & nowhere, she was divine.

THREE HOUSES

And look! my last, or
next-to-last, of three loved houses went.
Elizabeth Bishop

1. BENEFIT STREET

Up on the "almost pastoral" East Side
of town, where door after door bears the sign
of the Guardian Angel ("24-Hour

Surveillance & Security"), I duck
between the bas-relief Ionic columns
straddling the threshold of the Federal house

I've called mine ten years this April. Palm Sunday
come & gone yesterday, what as a child
I thought was "Monday" Thursday, then Good Friday
—days holy only as I remember them—

beat time at its own game. My future mortgaged,
I made my home in history inside
these four walls on a hill & said I could
imagine dying here, reborn at forty.

2. KYLE AVENUE

Again last night I sank up to my knees
into my native ground in Minnesota,
& it appeared my mother had bequeathed
to me our east-facing third house, complete

with the warm & fuzzy African violets
she raised in pots on a wrought-iron cart
inside the picture window, the room white
as my whole dream. After my father died

when I was twenty, vultures cleaned her out,
& she got hate mail like a ransom note
for selling to a black-&-white couple.

Moving, she scattered me to the four winds,
giving away ten years of baseball cards
& my Erector Set & Beat the Clock.

3. TWENTY-SECOND

Growing up, I celebrated the only
Easter warm enough to hunt eggs outside
looting the backyard of my mother's house,
where Nana hid for me a plastic bunny.
I squeezed its tail, breathing life into it,
& goosed it into jumping, pink like my pet
white rabbits' eyes I met at home each morning
behind the chicken wire of their blue hutch.

But soon a farmer came to take them all
off my father's hands, & I heard Grandpa
had gone like his black-spotted springer, Patsy,
the dark Easter of Joe DiMaggio's bat
& a ball autographed by Marty Marion.
Then I was ten, the house a memory.

MISSION

Because I wasn't ever any good
with my hands, a quaint Arts & Crafts oak sideboard
—hardwood from the heartland the sun has melted
the color & (to all appearances)

liquidity of honey—picks me up
like a metaphor, crossing categories
& taking me where I have never gone
since leaving my grandparents' house, the light

from their day (years before the first Great War)
ingrained in this gold heartwood here toward
the millennium. Dusting it with a palm,

as if in hopes the genius that conceived it
will rub off on me, I recall my fingers
are only good for measuring my words.

HARDBALL

After barrel-chested Earl Torgeson
(my father's favorite) & workmanlike
polite Bil! Tuttle (my mother's) had vanished
into the bus in the shadows outside
Comiskey Park, I stood
asking my idol, Al
Kaline, how to connect with the curve balls
I had already seen coming at twelve,
& he answered
shyly, a twenty-one-year-old crew-cut
blond "phenom" speaking from experience,
You have to find

your own way. It happened my way
would mean stealing a page from the curves' book
& winding down—as on a spiral stair—
into the ground along the lines
of the biggest curve imaginable,
which ends up in the dirt. No star, I knew
I'd never rise above the earth,
but sometimes I'd feel light-headed descending
on the spin my English put on each step
I took. In a word, I would make a virtue
of necessity, which, like rules,
freed me to play the game I'd choose.

AT LENGTH

Grounded, I watched late-breaking spring take off
without me in the yard. Nightly in March
a cardinal staking out his territory
under my bedroom woke me to the darkness
before dawn with his incessant wolf whistles.

On the eve of Easter a wave of black-masked
cedar waxwings, tail feathers tipped the gold
of each incipient Norway-maple leaf,
harrowed the earth, devouring as they went
fallen crab apples shriveled up like cherries.

Then, on May Day, the second oriole
of my life flashed across the lawn & dived
into the nettled, coral-flowering quince.
I took his fence-sitting mate for a vireo,
camouflaged as she was in drab olive.

Somewhere along the line, an orange-breasted
cock-of-the-walk a robin's size left me
speechless, & I looked him up—a towhee—
the way as a kid back in Minnesota
I passed long winters that kept spring on hold

leafing through a field guide. I came to know
birds I couldn't hope to see but started
repeating the names of—*indigo bunting,*
scarlet tanager—as a kind of song
I chanted silently, testing my wings.

COUNTRY SONG

Every shade of gray, your scales remind me
—though the scale is wrong—of a hoot owl's feathers,
& once, your black-lace wings
extended on a salt-&-pepper couch
where you snoozed camouflaged & I joined millions
cheering another summer's games in Rome
(the screened words courtesty of Olivetti),
I saw a dragonfly in you. Today,

when I awoke in a sweat at first light,
you started harping on what stings you deepest
morning to night. I had driven roads black
with ice, through fields blanked out by snow,
to my mother's failed heart again & cried
when my father was reduced to smoked meat . . .

You have your life mapped out for you, designed
so thoughtfully (down to your tail's point white
like the bird-lime ellipses finch & sparrow
chalk on slate-smooth bark to mark their absence)
that you become invisible to all
intents & purposes—save killer wasps?—
against this particular silver olive,
whose precious shade keeps the demon sun

from going to my head at noon. No Horace
swearing off wine, I still find my buzz comes
from you who drum your song into my head,
& soon I only hear my voice
singing my one note to myself, as I
likewise practice not being here, cicada.

LIFELINES

Wind scorches the dirty-blond earth
receiving the Temple
of Dionysus, whose columns shored up
by cement are marble
twenty centuries have weathered a cross
between the ashen trunks
of the still-standing olive trees
& their quicksilver leaves, as Teos returns
to dust surrounded by an endless grove

of mandarin oranges. When I dusted
myself off in the lime-green sea
opposite a beach gold in name
only, the water was so cold
it scalded me, the way I burned my tongue
licking a freezing monkey bar
gray as a pencil lead four decades back
below my mother's house deep in the City
of Lakes. Learning to hold my tongue early,

I hearkened to her stories of the figures
she'd cut as a girl skating into the dark,
scratching the surface of snow-dusted ice
lined like these moon-white
rectangles underfoot I now zigzag
digging up shadowy traces
of cryptic letters written
in stone—the black magic
that keeps souls alive when the sky caves in.

II

HYMN TO THE SUN

for Mutlu

I
Sleeping within earshot of the Aegean
once more, I forget where I am
a second & mistake the surf's white noise
for rain, unheard-of here

in summer. July Fourth, & the fireworks
all the apricot stars provide
leave me oohing & ahing like my mother
watching the real thing with me at North Commons

when I was eight. The child
conceived but inconceivable
in this house a year ago is two months
into his—& our—new life. Though he's present

in the flesh, he's still not to be believed.
His feet are the same color, size, & shape
as Eberhard erasers, perfect
for scuffing out any trace of his father's

footsteps. When birds applaud the sunrise, one big
coral rose unfolding, his blue eyes open
like morning glories, & he smiles, face breaking
into light like a sunflower.

II
Back at the Fisherman's Hotel in ancient
Halicarnassus for another summer
ten years ago, we woke up our first morning

& found our old boatman's
Antioch (named for his hometown) was missing
from the line-up of small craft all along

the shore. By noon we'd heard the news: asleep
or drunk, he'd fallen overboard last night
& drowned (he always joked about not swimming),

while his group of Americans below
slept peacefully & drifted until dawn.
That afternoon we watched men carry him,

wrapped in a green cloth like a movers' pad
crisscrossed with rope, & take turns shouldering
his dead weight through the streets for no more

than seven steps apiece—one for each day
of the weeks that run away with our lives—
in a kind of frantic dance that went on

until they got where they were bearing him,
& we continued, for the moment, walking
the opposite direction in the circle.

III
A cicada in the olive tree
outside our door pulses
like a fire alarm drilling kids in school.

Only this time
the fire is real: the sun
is burning us alive.

IV
On Bastille Day we ride into the city
on a heat wave & buy a graphite shade
("Elysian gray") of Renault, free
to write our own ticket in the future.

Every day "night condos," which is to say
cinder-block shanties owned by squatter's rights
the law grants whoever builds a roof
over his head before the sun rises

on it, climb higher up the mountainside
back of town, where they stand
like an ever-expanding house
of cards. Below, where Sparrows, Hawks, & Falcons

made by Fiat circle the poisoned bay,
a last Greek house with its marble facade
shining through the diesel haze is slated
to be crossed off the map by a new freeway.

V
Outside NATO's mirrored Southeast Command
Headquarters, the flags of many
nations stand saluting
the wind off the olive-
drab sea. One of the MP's on guard duty

squeezes his Uzi & smiles to himself
at his good luck to be watching
the legendary women of Izmir,
not waiting for the dust to rise
back in some Hittite village buried deep

in Anatolia. Meanwhile, a boy
with a rubber shoe on one foot
& a blue plastic sandal on the other
peddles the golden local variation
of sesame bagels stacked up to look

braided together on the big square tray
he balances on his head, round face freckled
as with those selfsame seeds, & a grown man
on a bike crates a honeycomb
of brown eggs through traffic

as though they were gold. On the quai
this morning, a guy hangs
over a freighter's side, painting the *s*
in *Tigris* the same blue
the water was just twenty years

ago & is today
in every last postcard of the modern
city, & lives in his own world as surely
as I misrepresent things putting them
in words, as if I were at home.

VI
Home after the birth, I entered our bedroom
alone & saw the handwriting
on the wall: the photographs nailed to it

were doomed. No more
shots one of us had taken of the other,
like the black-&-white you got of me staring

back at myself
in the Huntington's lily pond
—my shadow burned into a sheet of paper—

& no more uninhabited
landscapes like the sun-tanned blue vista
you froze in Cappadocia

of a potato field's lone tree
backed by a not-so-grand
canyon & Mount Argaeus, still snowed under

in August. We'd stopped our beige Hertz Renault
& stolen the season's last apricot
dangling from a branch no one, to our knowledge,

guarded, when a young man on a red bike
rode out of nowhere, eager
to talk. People were strong

around there, he said, but life was so hard
on his plateau that all of them wore out
by thirty-five, his voice as gravelly

as the mountain stream we'd heard when we lay
down beside it
earlier in the day, sick as tourists . . .

Thinking out loud, I told myself
we'd soon stick pictures of the newcomer
around the room & populate each future

view with him. For now, he lies & studies
an olive tree at sea in the wind, eyes
dancing, arms & legs churning away,

ecstatic. He sees leaf upon leaf flutter
like his small fingers in response, my own
ten fingers composing this candid picture.

VII
Diamond-blue Venus trapped
between the prongs

of tonight's white-gold crescent moon
can't hold a candle to the flash points

of the baby's eyes now as he examines
his hand like a jeweler sizing up

a precious stone, or an astronomer
discovering a star.

VIII
Each time the baby tugs
on his bottle, I feel his tongue

work the nipple like a sunfish
nibbling the bait at the end of my line

when I was small & fished
Leech Lake with my father.

IX
Turning my son's globe, I spot a flyspeck
at the center of the sky-blue Pacific:
Midway Island. It's one of those places

my father told us Boy Scouts all the war
stories about, everybody huddled
not around a campfire but in the glare

of a red Coleman that burned white
as the sun each day above the green lake
crawling with snaky weeds: Camp Many Point.

Moths dived into the flame like kamikazes
as he fleshed out his memories by thumbing
through *Destroyers*, his infallible bible.

Listening, we waited for our chance to gather
our own stories, all in good time.

X
A perfect circle, the red bull's-eye sun
glares through the white sea mist at ground level,
& the stooped melon man, dwarfed as ever
by his scarecrow-like sunflowers

hanging their doomed heads, stands
against it like a shadow once again
to count how many of his gold casabas
have ripened or been stolen overnight.

Here where melons are worth their weight in gold,
yesterday this earth-bronze skinflint refused
money for my birthday melon because
it looked too nearly perfect to be sold.

XI
Outside the door, a lamb on death row bleated
through the night like someone with the dry heaves.
In the morning he's sacrificed:
hogtied, blindfolded, throat slit, all the little
children suffered to watch (life not being
for the squeamish) & flinch perceptibly
as the lamb jerks his last & bleeds & bleeds,
Isaac's stand-in even at this late date

in history. Turning away, I hear
a rushing sound somewhere—water fanning
out across a yard's cracked dry earth? The eyes
beat ears as witnesses, writes Heraclitus:
red fire is sweeping through brown weeds nearby,
the one true god making its presence known.

XII
It always starts no bigger than a star,
a distant fire still the size of a spark,

& in full view mushrooms
into a blood-orange

fireball: the yellow sun rises
out of Asia, an H-bomb at ground zero.

All day the light
is one long blinding white nightmarish flash.

XIII
I dream of taking our small son to visit
your father's grave, an oversize bee box
topped with a round enameled porcelain
likeness of him not long before he died

at thirty-two. Above our heads the pines
that should be cypresses thrive on the lack
of water, old as death (not these
particular examples but their kind).

As I imagine remembering the scene,
our son is big enough to stand
in the dust & hang on my thumb the way
you clutched your father's thirty years before.

He slipped through your fingers into dark air
like a helium balloon you forgot
not to let go of as a little girl
leaving the fair at nightfall in his arms.

XIV
Last night I dreamed I'd lost you, & my life
was over, too. After all, you showed me
how to live, teaching me to look at things
I'd never seen. My grief at losing you
was like my panic at the thought
of going blind. Sharp-eyed
as the sun, you zero in on the sparrow's
every feather where, at one point, I didn't
even see a sparrow. Not a single
particular beneath
your notice, you quicken
each minute with your minute observations.
Lost in detail? Not on your life! Without
details, I'm lost & don't know where time goes.

Yesterday I paid a routine visit
to the village fountain—a roadside spigot
I'd have missed if I wesin't watching
for it—& saved the day
by opening my eyes to a mundane
vision. Surrounded by red plastic buckets
& silver pails, light-darkened faces lined
like the cracked end-of-August earth, three women

squatted on their haunches in ordinary
floral-print dresses—morning glories, orange
poppies, smoky tobacco leaves—& what
teeth they had left gleamed in the sun:
gold. The three Fates indicating my life
is flashing like a dream before my eyes?

XV
September means it's twenty years ago
this month I swam in salt water
here the first time in my life, hot springs veining
the marbled sea. Since then, I've dipped

into San Clemente's gold-flecked Pacific
& had the wind shocked out of me
by Maine's Atlantic at Acadia,
cold & clear as machine-made ice. The sea

isn't the enemy fresh water was
in Minnesota: there, I never thought
I'd learn to swim, dunked in chlorine while clinging
to the end of my rope

all winter &, each summer, thrown
into a lake, where sinking to the muddy
bottom was like imagining
polio. My salty

tears of fear & disappointment that showed
what others called my true colors in fact
proved I had it in me to stay afloat
when I found myself at sea in the world.

I only had to discover my points
of correspondence with it & I'd surface
in my element, buoyed by my inner
resources on the salt-white page.

XVI
Down on my hands & knees, nose to the ground,
I'm not a Muslim praying on a rug

like a bed of roses but a latter-day
fire-worshiper sniffing out a live

magenta carnation that took the whole
summer to bloom

under the sun, my be-all & end-all
touching all things.

XVII
Sunday is not the day the village worships
but a day of rest just the same: I wake
the gas man for a blue tube of propane,
& the postmaster wearing his all-business
grimace walks his little girl past the closed

new post office. Along the quai, the boats
anchored in the mirrored water still ride
on their dreams, while in the outdoor
restaurants the chairs have climbed up
on the tables & sleep, legs in the air.

In the Palace Barbershop, a boy reads
& sees how Arabs in a synagogue
yesterday blew twenty Istanbul Jews
to pieces, arms & legs in living color
on the graphic *New Century*'s front page.

XVIII
I was past forty when I harvested
my first olives this September, the tree
in question not a hundred yet & still
a baby. Spotting their black beauty marks

like periods that call an end
to their growing season, I went
out on a limb & reached the clustered fruits
peeping through the leaves like green eyes hidden

behind silver veils. The tree stands for peace
because it lives forever & its gifts
sustain so many morning, noon, & night.

Bent over backward now along the lines
of tonight's equinoctial gale, it gives
shape to the wind.

XIX
The first day of school, the village children
in black-&-white uniforms flock the narrow
streets like magpies. Heads bowed
above printed pages & eyes

trained on blackboards, they'll watch all color bleed
from the world as they learn by heart the rules
of grammar & the laws of number used
to quell the riot of impressions summer

incites in their senses. The sun, late riser
on this inaugural day
of fall, buries itself in clouds

that could be mountains, the kids left to stumble
through shadows if they want to see the light
letters & figures once sparked in my mind.

XX
Stars mist the blacked-out sky the last night
of September like gold dust carried off
by desert winds, one more summer's

treasure of days scattered
out of reach & reduced
to grains of sand the bully time is kicks

in my face. My head spins
with constellations drawn about as finely
as patterns in a Turkish rug that borders
on embroidery & grounds my eyes in what

lies under my nose. I have tried to weave
such a spell myself by tracing each thread
that ties me to the farthest star, a point
of light that comes to a point in my hands.

FADED KODACHROME

Every last leaf has fallen from the trees
around the darkened pond, a grit-scarred lens
that focuses the spotty washed-out blue
above. Dropping from the sky, a mallard
hits the skids as he applies the brakes,
stopping short on the water like a Corsair
landing, flaps down, on a carrier
in my father's day. My son falls for leaves
glinting like Lincoln pennies on the ground.
In the habit of finding signs
of resurrection everywhere
I turn, I mistake an airborne orange
beech leaf for a long-lived monarch
before I catch myself & think: *Too late.*

The woods have faded like a Kodachrome,
the way the farther I go back in album
time, the less colorful the characters
under the sun, till shades of gray
sink the family tree in mist & shadows.
Each step I take chasing my son
into the future puts that much more distance
between us in the book. Grabbing a minute,
we rest on what I teach him is a *stump,*
& the wind howling all around us barks
up any tree, right or wrong. Once, the light
was everything; now it's the wind,
hustling me off toward the day
when I will take my stand in black & white.

BURIAL GROUNDS

1. HISTORICAL CEMETERY

My mother always mourned the childlessness
of her lone brother for the simple fact
the family name would die with him, as if
she came from some unbroken royal line.
The baby boy who keeps my name alive
unbeknownst to her plays among the graves
of two-hundred-year-old strangers who've put
their hearts & souls into a copper beech
that shelters them from God's own sky at last,
but in the meantime here below
the elements have cost them all their names.

Walking the rows of upright white
tablets wind & rain have erased
& restored to their original state
of blank slates, my gleeful son pats them each
on the head, as though he were a grown-up
& they small children inching up on him.
From where I stand, the page-shaped slabs
I momentarily darken with my shadow
as with my name appear
thin as the paper I must trust
to outlast flesh & blood, let alone stone.

2. GRAY AREA

My infant son haunts the cemetery
& plays peekaboo with stones white
as the blank faces of so many swimmers
trying to keep their heads above water.

Watching him disappear
behind a certain marker, I make out
his given name writ large: a boy his age
who, I read, "unfortunately drown'd

in infancy" & whose
poor father, middle-aged like me two short
centuries ago, followed him I see
to an early grave the next year. The shallow

letters cut in rock look the same
tattletale-gray as my own name the sun
once filled with shadows as fast as a child
who'd learned to write could trace it in the snow.

3. BREAKING THE ICE

Visiting the dead, my son walks on water—
i.e., snow crusted with knife-edged
ice like the kind that almost took
the top of my head off when I went sailing
into it on my Flexible
Flyer &, picking myself up
off the floor of the valley, came home blinded
by tears & blood. Toward sundown
the growing shadows of the tapered stones
point accusing fingers at me
standing tall there, as a boy small enough
to play hide-&-seek among them
skates across the glaring surface
I break with every step of my cold feet.

THE SKY AS THE LIMIT

Thirty-five years ago I made this crossing
to Liberty Island, launched on the green
ferry toward dark. Rain cut down my view
of the weather-beaten Norwegian-copper
Statue with its aquamarine patina
my son at two calls a "big, big mommy."
Pointing to the sky, he holds up a make-
believe torch like the one that's drawn
all these shades of people
into the freezing air out here
on the cardboard-gray water, where we gather
at her feet, living in the past
that brought us together. As I look back

at the shore, the skyline with peaks & valleys
like an EKG doesn't measure up
to my child's vision of it I imagine
left a mark on me, the Empire State's
Eversharp half erased by the World
Trade Center's double towers shouldering
into the picture with their overstated
premise, "Bigness is all." Our hotel faced
Wanamaker's, & my mother went there
the night my father & I rode the El
to Ebbets Field, where I was scared to stand
up for my fellow visitors, the Reds,
in the top half of the seventh. They broke

into our red-&-black Rambler parked
below our room & stole my high-flown plans
for airplanes I drew up in hopes
of beating gravity with lines of force
arising, in my mind, from earth's
magnetic field. My parents tried
boosting my spirits with a blue-&-orange
wind-up plastic seaplane from the Waldorf,
but in the future I found other means
of transport, took new steps
to leave the ground behind, & put myself
on paper in a way that led to making
tall stories out of my short history.

COLD WAR

1. PAX AMERICANA

Digging out my toys kept under the bed
for years as if for this moment transports me
to 1953: my grandmother
opens her closet door & lets me in
on my Christmas present—not the ice skates

she's hinted at & a gift-wrapped shoebox
points to, but an unassembled sky-blue
tin replica ("Made in Japan," it writes)
of a B-29 of A-bomb fame
with friction wheels that in turn spin the four

propellers with a racket so God-awful
my little boy is scared to death & reaches,
instead, for the orange cast-iron model
of an International Harvester
tractor a dealer gave me for the asking

that summer, when I visited New York
Mills with her & discovered in the sunlit
attic of an abandoned farmhouse there
a bomb shell tattooed with Oriental
characters, a forgotten war souvenir

I carried home safely on a Greyhound
& used to pin down papers in a breeze
as I grew older & began myself
scratching my living from lead-black furrows
under the shadow of the clear blue sky.

2. PRIVATE LICENSE

After church when my father stopped with me
at Lou & Benny's drugstore for unfiltered
Tareytons & Palmer House, I'd kneel down
to thumb *Collier's* & *Look*, their glow-in-the-dark
glossy paper glare ice under the new

fluorescent lights. My Army-green parka
insulating me from the endless cold,
head shaved flat as if for boot camp, I searched
for an exit from this world all the war
comics with their black-eyed "Russkies" & "gooks"

failed to show me. Well-versed in how a lowly
creature like me could never hope to get
beyond my desires, I worshiped images
artists rendered of daddy-longlegs-style
lunar landers, dying to wear a halo

of pure oxygen like those boxy figures
drawn running around with upended fishbowls
on their heads, & I pretended to withstand
a string of G's as I escaped earth's pull
—steering, I imagined, by the joystick

of my father's Cessna—for the moon's orbit
& gladly fell under the page-white spell
of its reflected light, as if I knew
even then I couldn't live anywhere
except on the margins, at one remove.

SETTING OUT

for my son

You won't remember how we walked tonight
after you cried, your *Little Golden Book
of Planets* under your arm, "Let's go out
on the earth & see what

is there!" Under the moon you'd found egg-shaped
with only a handful of words
last year, owls—you spotted
two fledglings in the yard one morning, dead—

announced their unseen presence with a sound
(a hiss alternating with a deep sigh)
like your heavy breathing
when you sleep off another long hard day,

& crickets lying low
rolled their *r*'s around us in the grass,
while the stars I saw highlight the Big Dipper
struck you as flashes in the black pan

I use to cook you flapjacks every Sunday
& my DAR grandmother always swore
her Conestoga-driving forefathers
lugged west. When in the end

you summed up the world so far—"On the earth
are owls & crickets, & in the sky, stars"—
I listened to how still things were
above the undercurrent of the sea

coming & going like my blood I heard
slosh back & forth on an echocardiograph
before your time, my irregular heart
a weathered craft straining at its frayed line.

WHOLE LIFE

When my son waters down strays with his long-
range squirt gun from the patio, my father
aims my air rifle at the tom that slaughtered
the robins in our weeping willow his last

summer. The nights his heartache kept sleep
at a distance, I awoke, too, & listened
as the boy he'd been watched a Minnesota

River suckhole swallow his friend, & witnessed
Doc Duclos raised from his own filth each April,
the squaw he'd shacked up with gone at the thaw.

Just as the stories that my father told
let him round off his life, his origins
as close to him as he'd come to his end,
the tales I spin this way bring me full circle.

SECOND LANGUAGE

> *. . . love begins at the point when a woman*
> *enters her first word in our poetic memory.*
> Milan Kundera

The smallest green chameleon
gone like a flick
of its tongue returns me

to our beginnings
& brings back the first time
twenty-five years ago you ran

across the English word for it
& asked me what it meant.
When I explained it stood

for change, you wondered
what would become of us,
& I heard myself say

for my part I would go
on loving you, language
I'd never used in all my days.

THE SUMMER HOUSE

Dalyan, Turkey, 1990

1. BACK IN ASIA MINOR

Another year time has taken the measure
of space, & I raise a golden blond Venus
to your return to home ground, as the sun
in a child's eyes starts to bleed into shady

Chios. Spring gets bloody in the Aegean:
everywhere you look, traces of crimson
poppies spatter the fields, as if all Hades
had risen bodily from God's green earth.

From a distance, the first white sailboat testing
June's silver waters is a butterfly
lighting, at nightfall, in a smoky olive.

Crickets break out their tiny castanets,
warming up to keep time, like me, one more
summer. What, but love, has taken me this far?

2. GENETIC CODE

My son tells me I'm his "living night light."
Whatever he may mean by it, I know
that I could gaze at him all night, as if
I were my father or my mother back
from the dead to watch over one they never
got to see in life. Neither can I stop
fearing the worst for him even in dreams.

Maybe I'm like "poppies in the dust,"
as he calls those tongues of flame wavering
out of the sand pile a neighbor dug into
last fall, mixing cement for his late father's
memorial. Because no one here but comes
& goes like the wind, too, I light the way
with words black as poppy seeds dropped in passing.

3. UNSCHEDULED FLIGHT

At dawn I go down to Homer's Aegean
& find blue swallows cutting figure eights
above a field of yellow gorse, purple
burdock, oxeye daisies, various shades
of starry eyebright, yarrow, & wild carrot.
Scything the air, they live on what no mortal
eye can see, & take me back twenty years
to the Piazza Michelangelo
in Florence at dusk, when I saw these birds
thriving on the invisible as spirits
rising & falling above Dante's Arno,
tails forked like the gold nibs of Grandpa's
fountain pens I dipped into at eight
& filled with Sheaffer's ink blue as swallows.

4. DESCENT

When I see how fast the sun disappears
behind the mountains of Chios, gone all
at once like an orange rolled off the edge
of a table, I begin to grasp the speed
I'm flying through my days, with faith in nothing
but the light. That reminds me of the story

of Johnny, Arthur, Tony—RAF
fly-boys who stopped on their last leave & tossed me
into the air at my Welsh grandfather's
before they flew back home, only to vanish
in fog returning from a German raid
or meet with friendly fire crossing the Channel,
nobody there to catch them when they fell.
They swim before my eyes, names black as floaters.

5. INDEPENDENCE DAY AT THE EMPIRE'S END

Forty-some years, & I remember waking
up on the Fourth all unable to wait
for night & the blue-&-white-checked firecrackers
my shadowy father tossed off in the dark

with a bang, the gold sparklers I trailed flaming
like comets as I ripped through the universe
of the black yard starred with lightning bugs I got
my feet wet catching in a Skippy jar,

& the red shooting stars of Roman candles
I scanned the sky for like a volunteer
out to ID Tupolev bombers zooming
down from Canada below the DEW line . . .

Tonight's burnt-powder smell of summer rain
through a screen door is only settled dust.

6. ESTATE PLANNING

In my dream garden I would plant an olive,
its owl-eyed leaves keeping my eyes open
to the light's dark side; a pomegranate's blossoms
would reproduce for me each spring that certain
red or orange of the Bakelite handles
on my first knives & forks in Eden Prairie;
an almond tree, its halo of shed flowers
recalling the ghostly circle a horse drew
on Konya's threshing floor; an apricot
mooning me with its freckled little sunburnt
buttocks; Venus-pale jasmines with the scent
that brings back my last night in the Golden State;
& then a cypress's eternal flame,
quill-shaped & black as ink, to mark my grave.

7. SUNDAY PAGAN

This is the kind of day I'll die recalling.
Flush with the atmosphere at last, the air
the same temperature as my body now,
I warm to a sea neither blue nor green—
not sky or earth but something in between,
the holy water that baptizes me
in the one life of the four elements.

On the same wavelength as the sun, I burn
as if I had all the time in the world,
summer convincing me I'm of a piece
with things in spirit for a day or season.
Intensified, the light transfixes me,
as when I feel a spell is coming on
& fall into a trance, a little song.

8. REMAINING LIGHT

A dreamy-eyed gold colt born yesterday
sniffs his first mustard thistle gingerly,
seeing how the chestnut mother he milks
wolfs down one after another nearby.

When he ducks the smart Maxxum I have aimed
at him & seeks refuge in her shadow,
the perfect white diamond between his eyes
catching what remains of the light gives him

away. Almost out of time, I picture
my son, already into his fourth summer,
hugging his tow-headed friend & beaming
against the background of this leggy creature,

as the sun leaves the field to growing darkness
& all I envision fades to black words.

9. DOUBLE TALK

When I pluck my son an olive leaf—one side
so purely silver the light turns it white,
the other wine-bottle-green—he flips me
a pink palm & the tanned back of a hand.

Under the shadow of our being history
tomorrow, what's made of the August earth grows
unbearably bright: knobby little heads
of garlic trailing clods of dirt & hung

together with gold twine; melons lemon-
yellow strung from almonds like paper lanterns;
& oil ink-spotted olives secreted
away the green gold of last summer's sun.

The darkness in me also sees the light
on white leaves in my lined exercise book.

10. FISHING VILLAGE FAREWELL

The sea the color of petroleum,
waving white flags of surrender, proclaims
this summer's fall. Across the gulf, the island
lost in the mist of distance since the solstice
closes in. September, & time to clear
out, a chill in the blood & war once more
in the air. I'll never finish horse-starved
Xenophon's journey home through Kurdistan,
I tell myself, & capture my son flanked
by two friends in a parting shot as they
glare back into the last of the sun, light
catching them like a sultana-gold net
some fisherman enmeshed in his lines mends
all afternoon beside the still backwaters.

IV

GRAPHIC SCENES

1. MOTHER TONGUE

When I was growing up, my mother lip-
synched everything I said, as if I played
Charlie McCarthy to her Edgar Bergen
on an "Ed Sullivan Show" tape reversed.

Reading her lips, which trembled as they did
bristling with pins whenever she cut out
a midnight-blue pattern, I watched my words
come back to haunt me like an echo made

visible. Like those lettered souls dumbstruck
Augustine saw mouth Scripture silently,
she'd repeat my syllables to herself

as gospel. Shadowing my speech, she taught me
to listen while I spoke, so that one day
I'd talk like this, without moving my lips.

2. TYPEFACE

Each time the sun sinks hibiscus-red, shrivels
up to a point, & shows its true colors
as a star, my heart drops with it, as if
my day in the sun withered away in a day.

My mother wouldn't let it set on her,
who maintained a year-round tan in the face
of the fly-by-night Minnesota sun,
never once resorting to Florida

or a sun lamp. In her words, she "got black,"
lying in the snow in her copper-toned
bikini I mistook for skin at twelve
before I could turn back around the corner.

Maybe I learned from her to bend the light
to my purposes, blackening as I speak.

3. TRANSPORT

I felt as weightless when, at one, my son
took his first steps across the living room
into my arms, the flowers underfoot
a wedding gift two decades old still blooming
like the garden that May, as when, four years
later, he threw himself into the sea
today & trusted it would hold him up
the way the ground had underwritten him.

The joy of such moments is like the high
I get rising above the gravity
of my situation by engraving it
on paper, leaden feet climbing the ladders
firmly planted in darkness letters are
above the flatline on my horizon.

4. WHITE WATER

At seventeen I was already writing
on water at the Aquatennial,
practicing my J-stroke to keep my Grumman
in line as I canoed the Mississippi
from Paul Bunyan country south to St. Paul.
Cass Lake Chippewas harvested wild rice
under my nose, almost invisible,
& one night my father showed up in camp
dressed by my mother after his heart trouble:
Bermudas with knee socks, not his trademark
weekend khakis, & soft shoes I'd soon fill
instead of black canvas high-tops (Converse).
I had only begun throwing out lines
to try & save souls from water's white rush.

5. MAN OF LETTERS

Blank scrolls of waves unfolding at his feet,
a five-year-old scratches his name with sandstone
on tablets he no sooner fishes out
of the water than the sea wipes them clean,
just as the dizzy smoke-blowing pilot
overhead chalks backward letters on the sky
high-flying wind erases at the speed
breath clouds evaporate from a mirror:

who doesn't burn to leave his mark? As good
as fifty, my days spent translating myself
into indelible ink & vice versa,
I can't tell my razor-point's strokes from blood
now that my signature resembles nothing
more than a heartbeat on an EKG.

6. MIRACLE MILE

My father never thought that he would die
of natural causes but always believed
he'd meet his end on the road, seeing how
he drove a hundred thousand miles a year.
Yet he beat the odds on an accident
only to get blind-sided by his heart,
sitting in his forest-green La-Z-Boy
& watching "Gunsmoke" in his oak-lined den.

My mother reported on his deathbed
he tried, cool to the last, to help the doctors
find his pulse. That's when Brother Patrick prayed,
speeding me there in his blue Malibu,
& I clung to lines I knew by heart, starting
to drum up a pulse to bring back my father.

7. MURMUR

Pressing my ear to my only child's heart,
I hear steps approach from the past, forebears
out of breath but standing up to be counted
all the same, while other feet stampede
into the future minus me & recede
as to a drumbeat, the way he grew smaller
the time his mother took him for his first walk
away from home, down the street to the corner,
& left me watching from the door, looking
out from the threshold as through the wrong end
of a telescope. But then my head echoes
with footsteps constantly, mothers & fathers
putting their feet down in accents & stresses
that, as far as I can tell, come from my heart.

8. IN STITCHES

In her embroidered history, my Norwegian
grandmother's Swedish father was the king
of tailors. As if no bloodline dropped a stitch,

my mother arrived to pick up the thread
& sewed all her own clothes from Vogue patterns
she pinned to the whole cloth that she devised

her outfits from. Sitting still at her knee,
I watched her tap her foot to keep the Singer
humming above my head, & grew to suit
myself, contriving to dress my form in such

tailored threads as I could afford. Whenever
her handiwork would fit her like a glove,
she'd laugh & say she felt she wasn't wearing
a stitch. In time I'd be the man clothes made.

9. MEASURED RESPONSE

The katydids amount to the loose change
my uncles & my father, fingers smoothing
his monogrammed penknife thin as a dime,
jingled in the deep pockets of the baggy
suit pants they wore to my grandmother's Sunday
dinners in the Fifties, while the crickets
are cops blowing the whistle on the summer,
preserving order at the seasons' march.

Picking raspberries on Autumn Road late
this afternoon equaled tweaking erect
nipples in a dream, & my son came to choose
blueberries grown as inky as the sky
soon went. My erratic heart keeps me awake
all night, as I try not to miss a beat.

10. BLOOD SAMPLE

A fallen maple leaf time's stained as red
as the Zinfandel my heart doctor keeps
bleeding from my arm brings home the meaning
of the "veins" on it I show my son. Young

enough to be my grandson, still a year
from learning how to figure & to read,
he asks with all his heart, "Why are numbers
more powerful than letters but not as sweet

& pretty as the alphabet?" Speaking
for myself, I say words—black as they are—
vein the "leaf" at hand as if with blood,

the way a reader gone back to fine print
from staring down the sun faces the "color
of sunset" my boy calls prenatal darkness.

11. CARDIOGRAM

Chances are good my number will be up
before my kindergarten son ever
graduates from high school, my doctor hints,
given my scores on my latest blood test.

In the past, she let me have the Bible's full
threescore & ten, but now the numbers tell,
she says, a different story: I am twice
as likely as your average man to fall

victim to my heart. When you factor in
family history, forget it; my ticker
is a time bomb, as if I didn't know.

In matters of the heart I always go
strictly by the numbers, after all,
counting down to the certain end of the line.

12. ECHO

The med technician screening my off-beat
heartbeat tells me no two hearts sound the same.
My aortic valve pumps sporadic bursts
of automatic fire, & my tricuspid
gurgles *swift, swift* as if on its deathbed,
each word maybe its last. Unscarred, my mitral
coughing up blood is a boy with the croup.

Then she changes her tune, if not her mind,
saying all hearts are pretty much alike,
& shows me my heart going up in blue
& red flames that turn to smoke whenever
I take too deep a breath, sighing because
my life is on the line in this dark room,
my crazed heart bared & scanned for images.

MUSE

When she parades her new glad rags
before me, I instinctively
reach out to her & take the cloth
between my thumb & forefinger,
like a woman buying dry goods
anywhere in the world or like

my father in his tailored suits
showing the line of "rags" he sold,
given as he was to feeling
the nub of each material
he wrote orders for & carried
in thumb-size square swatches displayed

inside the tall black sample
cases with brass casters that,
after he couldn't raise his beige
Schick electric at Methodist
Memorial, he'd run out of breath
lifting up a curb. His age then,

I try to keep one step ahead
of his heart & pound the pavement
four miles three times a week, staying
even with his grandson madly
pedaling his Huffy on the road
to outdistancing me at last.

Except my father's ghost always
catches up with me whenever
she shimmers into view decked out
like new, & I begin to weave
& stitch the fabric of my life
together, fingering rag bond.

VISIONARY COMPANY

Last night when our son said, "The two of you
are beautiful," we knew he wasn't falling
for how the shadows at our candle-lit

dinner for three erased the lines the years
have raked across our faces, but perhaps
buttering us up & learning to trade

words for love. Putting myself in his place,
I sat back at the right hand of my father,
who manfully watched me play his opposite

versus his understudy, as when, hair
silvered for *King Lear*'s Kent like his, it happened
I kissed him good-bye on the mouth for good,

& across the blond table from my mother,
whose blue shadow box hung over my head
& in whose teal-flecked eyes I could do no wrong,

wrong as I was in so much that I did
or failed to do, like telling her the fall
she died I'd be a father in the spring.

I saw my parents vanish in the time
it took our candle to burn down to nothing
—both, to my mind, beautiful in that light.

MY FATHER'S CARS

for John

First he drove his father's '17 Dodge
as a boy no bigger than you, then Fords
—I am going by the 3x5 list
he wrote me at the dinner table just
one month before he died, the notepaper
Roberts Company's (their motto "Exclusive
But Not Expensive," their logo white gloves

under a black top hat)—not distinguished
by model ("T" or "A") but simply numbered
'18 & '23. Two more Dodges
('25 & '26) intervened
before another Ford—a '27—
ended his druggist father's run of cars:
the Crash reduced his GM stock to paper.

Owing what he was owed, he'd still afford
a '31 Studebaker my father
used weekends, home from a school that banned driving
to help out at the fountain Saturdays.
Taking his life in his hands after college,
he traveled as a seed man all across
the Mississippi Delta, & sold drugs

to Great Plains Walgreens, in nine Chevrolets
& a '36 Ford. One time, he said,
he had to shake off a man with a gun
who'd jumped onto his running board (his own
pistol locked up in what I called the glove
"department"), & he "*wrecked*" (emphasis his)
a '35 on a back road outside

New Orleans. In the hospital he fattened
on Cajun fried chicken—his twenty-seven
wings at a sitting set, he claimed, a record—
while he recovered from the leg he'd broken
pinned beneath the car all night in a ditch,
hearing the other guy moan till daybreak
brought a cotton wagon & a black man

whose mule team rescued him in time. It seems
he tried to forget a second '35
he went back & squeezed in between the lines
with this notation: "Dallas—also wrecked."
Scaling the Bighorns in a '38,
he took my mother west to Sheridan,
Wyoming, where the Cheyennes christened him

"Sitting Bear." He changed horses to a Mercury
before a '40 Plymouth, named for where
(he'd laugh) his mother dreamed her people landed.
Two more Merc's alternated with two Chevys:
the one before Pearl Harbor saw him through
the Armistice Day blizzard with my mother,
when they were trapped in it outside Sioux City

overnight, & the other's open door
entered the wedding picture of him looking
wolfish as he ushers in his bride,
leaving St. Olaf's on St. Valentine's.
Except on Monday they will dodge the bullet
of his draft notice & honeymoon pushing
straight through to Omaha, where he'll enlist

his fifty-inch chest & off-the-scale weight
in the Navy's service. When three years later
my mother joins him on Nob Hill, his ship
in drydock & his Purple Heart already
put behind him for me to unearth down
the basement & dust off when he is gone,
he'll guide another '42 Mercury

—black this time & for official business
only, like delivering telegrams
that stop the heart & give rise to gold stars—
north to Oregon where, a uniformed
line officer, he'll get chewed out by small
people when he asks a waitress for butter
(his wealth of guns, they'll judge, has made it scarce).

You want to hear me call the roll of all
his wheels, because you're five & learned to talk
rattling off the names of the cars you ogled
when you found your sea legs walking the city.
It turns out that you memorized their emblems,
like Mitsubishi's cloverleaf you spied
on tins of 3 Diamonds tuna your class

presented those who had nothing. Each can,
round like a zero, recalled the name
of the same company's plane that zeroed in
on my father's empty stateroom aboard
the *U.S.S. Morris* & blew his khakis
sky-high before they ended up flying
inside-out from his sinking destroyer's mast,

their black-stenciled serial number brought to light.
Picking up the story, ABC News
carried it on the cherry RCA
my grandmother enshrined above her icebox
(a Frigidaire would be her spoils of battle),
my mother there seeing the one-year-old
I was grow up without a father now.

This is where I come in after the war.
He bought & sold in rapid-fire succession
a '46 Ford & a navy Olds
I knew, they told me, as an "O-mobile"
(already letters said it all for me)
among the various makes Detroit shipped out
as fast as I could finger them on sight,

the way he'd studied silhouettes in order
to eyeball Japanese vessels from the bridge
the instant they had darkened his horizon
& crossed his field of 20/10 vision.
I can still see him park under our oak
his twelve-cylinder '46 Zephyr
with the first-ever automatic windows,

which froze up on him in the "down" position
when the temperature hit bottom near Bismarck.
After two Fords & one more Mercury,
where to this day I'm standing on the floor
behind my parents in the brushed front seat
I grab because I'm scared the car will split
in half & cut me off from them for good,

my mother in the '49 black Lincoln
broadsided a guy running a stop sign.
Riding shotgun, I lucked out & was thrown
under the dash, my jigsaw-puzzle map
of all the states beside me blown to pieces
like rainbow confetti. Though next year's Dodge
has managed to survive in a photograph

she snapped of me posed in the snow, an echo
of my tall father in an overcoat,
galoshes, & (I know) a brown fedora,
I recall as clearly the pea-green '50
Mercury came to life when, for blocks,
every car went dead those breathtaking mornings
of thirty-five below it spirited me

to school—the tangerine buses failed to start—
so that I wouldn't miss a thing but learn
to cross my t's & dot my i's, minding
my p's & q's no matter what the weather,
only to buy time now, fighting a holding
action (see Korea) to save a lost
continent. From this distance, his cars look small

as your Matchboxes or my Tootsietoys,
not to mention my Porsche convertible
imported from divided Germany
I wound up with a flat black key at six,
its color on the borderline of orange
& red. Standing in our garage, my mother's
hand-painted crimson tulips on the door,

my father compared our first second car
—a cream-&-powder-blue '49 Nash—
to an "upside-down bathtub" of the kind
with feet my grandparents' old house had then.
But when the Fifties squared rounded-off corners,
he bought a '53 American
& the '54 Rambler that sold me on

Howard Johnson's hot dogs & coffee ice cream,
starting in Ohio on our drive east
the summer I would turn eleven. Early
one July morning I opened my eyes
in the front seat become a hide-a-bed,
& scowled out the window at Boston's Common,
which memory keeps as green as Fenway's grass.

I'm getting way ahead of myself here.
The '52 Pontiac took us west
as far as the Black Hills, & my black Lab
ran scared when life-size dinosaurs arose
from the Badlands. Shot on Calamity
Jane's grave, I'm dressed as you'll remember me—
in black from hat to boots, like the Cisco Kid

or Zorro, never in the good-guy's white
like Roy Rogers when I envisioned him
on stage through the auditorium's gray haze,
or the Lone Ranger when I shook his hand
at Powderhorn. I visited the bar
in Deadwood's ghost town, where blackjack-playing
Wild Bill Hickock got ambushed from behind.

Death was in the air the Saturday night
I woke to Mr. Daley, who kept coming
home from bars with black eyes, preaching salvation
off in the kitchen, & I listened hard
to my mother quizzing him about heaven
before she pulled her red '51
Ford convertible out from under me

& disappeared into silence until
after church in the morning, when my dad
told me her father—your namesake—had died.
Sleeping in his room two summers ago,
I'd been awakened by street noise below:
stifling at home, the whole house was leaving
for floats at Broadway's A&W

in the '51 Pontiac, its amber
Indian-head hood ornament a copy
of my father's antique penny I would save
in the clear-plastic box with buffalo
nickels & inflated Civil War dollars
thieves lifted, together with his wood-handled
Colt .45, over his dead body.

He made the used-car dealer eat his lemon
of a '50 Ford, but talked himself out
of a back seat for his black '54
Ford business coupe. The '56 sedan
let me track the Tigers through a series
in Chicago, where black kids my own age
asked us for change to watch our car. The next

October, when my ill-starred family
glided into our driveway in our new
'58 Ford Fairlane three shades of beige
late at night, we heard the voices of Gabriel
Heater & Walter Winchell grow quiet
before the advent of the first sputnik
left us huddled around the dial's glow;

the stars we rifled with our eyes felt closer
than the gravel beneath our tires. Soon I'd leave
our lowered turquoise-&-azure '55
Chevy Bel Air with dual exhausts & spots
idling at the curb in suburban darkness,
as I walked Kathy to her door, who'd lost
her parents in a traffic accident.

Badgered by me, my father would consent
to the red '61 VW
I crawled home in through a Belt Line snowstorm
from the ICU where he pulled for me.
His years as many as the cars he'd driven,
the good life proved too much of a good thing—
T-bones, Jim Beam, & Herbert Tareytons.

As if he knew when he'd run out of space,
his bottom line was not the '63
Chrysler Imperial he wanted black
but the white Dart with red interior
he'd had to settle for & I steered back
from the hospital without him one last time.
Now I'll be with you when you take that journey.

GOLDEN AGE

1. BLACK FEET

My son carries home from school a tale
of an Indian boy abandoned in the snow
& warned by his strict father not to follow
the tracks he'd leave behind while disappearing

for three months. Winter's coming; my son hopes
I'll never leave him to his own devices,
whether pointing arrows or weaving snowshoes
out of white-tailed deer sinews & yew branches.

A bold-lettered bumper tells us Indians
discovered America—except they left
no words to show where they had come & gone.

If all goes well, it will be a cold day
when I depart, my footprints here for him
to trace where I went, black under the sun.

2. WHITE SPACE

After the fireworks of maples exploding
in bursts of red & yellow like the sparks
that rained down at dark to commemorate
Columbus Day, only some gold leaf stuck
to a birch tree or a gingko, wind-quickened
like a butterfly glinting in late sun,
reminds me of the many rooms in autumn's
mansion, now an abandoned haunted house.

Halloween's half-moon seemingly observed
fall was halfway home to the longest night.
Trick-or-treating, my boy witnessed a father
wielding a bat against evil spirits;
in my day, I saw my parents masquerade
as the ghosts they've become, white as sheets still.

3. STUDY

The fall when I was ten & lay marooned
in a sickbed, I begged my grandmother
(no Grandma Moses) to paint me the golden

valley outside my window. For the first
& last time, she took up my watercolors,
composed a picture of decomposition.

This Sunday morning in my fiftieth
November, the gold Norway maple out
my window renders it stained glass that colors
my view of my heartsick father, fifty,

keeping his finger on his pulse & gilds
the page where I record the beats I count
on my fingers, taking down my heart's message
as gilt yields to letters branching out black.

4. FOOT BRIDGE

I get my cues from nature but am not
only nature's boy this freezing November
anniversary of my mother's death.

She who'd taken three men's hands & shown them
out of this world died alone like her mother,
a neighbor finding her "as cold as ice"—

cold as today. I couldn't face her body
under a sheet, trusting whoever lifted
the gold chain from her neck gave her a name.

Although my son would have me bury him
with gold leaves in the yard, I cross on foot
black water where the sky itself founders,

emptied of clouds but not the smoky souls
no less visible than the air I breathe.

ON BLACK ISLAND

1. SHELLING

My mother shadows me this New Year's Day
& looks over my shoulder as I comb
the beach in her adopted Florida.
As if I've seen a ghost, my hair is turning
white like the ibis with his flamingo bill
or the snowy egret with his cowlick,
pollen-gold eyes, & yellow-starfish feet.

Like him, I pick my way along white sand,
not among shells one overlooks who's found
no names for them, but among words I learned
from her. She made the buried world a treasure
visible to me, unveiling turbans
& minarets, tulips, olives, & milky
figs, augurs & good-as-gold alphabets.

2. NUMBERS

When my mother went up in smoke, rising
into Orlando's burnt-orange atmosphere,
I drove my fiery Alamo Horizon
till the Bee Line dead-ended in the glare
off Cape Canaveral. There on the tarred
& feathered shore, I scanned the blank Atlantic,
wind throwing my words back at me like ashes.

Seven years later I face the music
here on the other side. Going on six,
my child sees it rain diamonds on the Gulf,
& up against a sky sheeted with clouds
the palm fronds' blades scissor thin air, like me
grasping at straws trapping spirits between
my writing hand's thumb & first two digits.

SCORING

Six in the spring, my son's become obsessed
with boundaries overnight & seems determined
to fence himself in with four orange cones
like those that form dotted lines on highways
around car accidents, breakdowns, & road
repairs, using them to stake out end zones
on his imaginary Soldier Field

in the backyard. He once thought nothing out
of bounds who now plows across the goal lines
in the snow, the ball tucked in his armpit
instead of running with it like a kid
"stealing a watermelon"—in the words
my bear-like father would have told him also,
teaching him how to hit paydirt. I learned

my limits from my grandfather: standing
outside the five-&-dime on North Broadway,
he wouldn't set foot on its squeaky floor
beneath its slow-motion ceiling fans
to buy me a car, pleading poverty
despite (in my view) the Northwestern Bank
across the street, & thereby saved the day.

Just as my boy has come to concentrate
his energies by playing games with rules
& in the fall will go to school to find
letters only spell words others can read
if they are written down between blue lines,
I force myself to live within my means
& count my syllables to make them count.

PERMANENT INK

The sun shrinking to a vanishing point
of light gives me a jolt, like the small shock
the faulty wiring of my heart
shoots through it now
& then. Where a little child sees an *o*

for *orange*, I find a black hole
my days feed into, one by one, the way
words sentenced to stand together for life
come down to a period's needle-eye zero
nothing passes through. In the next breath

sparks fly across the sky
I gaze into as if wishing
upon my future in a shining well
of ink, & the scene goes dark as these letters
suffused, in their time, by so many shades.